Neighborhood Safari

Coyotes

by Dalton Rains

FOCUS READERS
PIONEER

www.focusreaders.com

Copyright © 2025 by Focus Readers®, Mendota Heights, MN 55120. All rights reserved. No part of this book may be reproduced or utilized in any form or by any means without written permission from the publisher.

Focus Readers is distributed by North Star Editions:
sales@northstareditions.com | 888-417-0195

Produced for Focus Readers by Red Line Editorial.

Photographs ©: Shutterstock Images, cover, 1, 4, 6, 8, 10, 12, 14, 17, 21; iStockphoto, 18

Library of Congress Cataloging-in-Publication Data
Names: Rains, Dalton, author.
Title: Coyotes / by Dalton Rains.
Description: Mendota Heights, MN: Focus Readers, [2025] | Series: Neighborhood safari | Includes bibliographical references and index. | Audience: Grades K-1
Identifiers: LCCN 2023053413 (print) | LCCN 2023053414 (ebook) | ISBN 9798889981732 (hardcover) | ISBN 9798889982296 (paperback) | ISBN 9798889983408 (pdf) | ISBN 9798889982852 (ebook)
Subjects: LCSH: Coyote--Juvenile literature | Coyote--Anatomy--Juvenile literature | Coyote--Behavior--Juvenile literature | Coyote--Life cycles--Juvenile literature
Classification: LCC QL737.C22 R364 2025 (print) | LCC QL737.C22 (ebook) | DDC 599.77/25--dc23/eng/20231222
LC record available at https://lccn.loc.gov/2023053413
LC ebook record available at https://lccn.loc.gov/2023053414

Printed in the United States of America
Mankato, MN
082024

About the Author

Dalton Rains is a writer and editor from Minnesota.

Table of Contents

CHAPTER 1
Hidden Hunter 5

CHAPTER 2
Body Parts 9

CHAPTER 3
Night Sight 13

Clever Coyotes 16

CHAPTER 4
A Coyote's Life 19

Focus on Coyotes • 22
Glossary • 23
To Learn More • 24
Index • 24

Chapter 1

Hidden Hunter

A coyote creeps through tall grass. A rabbit hops nearby. The coyote follows it. Then it leaps toward the rabbit. The coyote has its meal.

Coyotes can live in many different places. Some live in forests or deserts. Others live near cities. Coyotes usually live without **shelter**. But they move into dens when they have pups.

Fun Fact

Coyotes' dens may be under rocks or inside trees.

Chapter 2

Body Parts

Coyotes have big ears. The animals also have sharp claws. They have sharp teeth, too. Coyotes use their strong **jaws** to rip meat.

Coyotes are **mammals**. They have fur all over their bodies. Some coyotes have light-brown fur. Others are almost black. Their fur can be long and heavy. Coyotes also have bushy tails.

Fun Fact

Coyotes are about as large as medium-sized dogs.

Chapter 3

Night Sight

Coyotes' fur acts as **camouflage**. The fur helps coyotes hide. The fur also helps coyotes stay warm during winter.

Large ears help coyotes hear **prey**. Long noses help coyotes smell other animals. Coyotes have strong eyes, too. They help coyotes hunt at night.

Fun Fact

A coyote can run more than 40 miles per hour (64 km/h).

That's Amazing!

Clever Coyotes

Coyotes are smart animals. They have **adapted** to different areas. Most coyotes used to live in **prairies** and deserts. Now, they also live in forests and mountains. They even live in cities. Coyote **populations** continue to grow.

Chapter 4

A Coyote's Life

Coyotes **mate** in the winter. Pups are born in a **litter**. At first, the pups stay in their den. Parents find food. They spit it into the pups' mouths.

After a few weeks, pups start finding food for themselves. Males may leave their family after six to nine months. Coyotes begin to mate after two years. Some mates stay together for the rest of their lives.

Fun Fact In the wild, most coyotes live for six to eight years.

Life Cycle

- Coyotes mate during winter.
- Female coyotes move into dens and give birth in spring.
- Both parents help feed pups.
- Pups can go out of the den after a month.
- Some pups move away within a year.

FOCUS ON
Coyotes

Write your answers on a separate piece of paper.

1. Write a sentence describing the main idea of Chapter 2.
2. Would you want a coyote to live near your home? Why or why not?
3. How long do most coyotes live in the wild?
    - A. a few weeks
    - B. six to nine months
    - C. six to eight years
4. Why might coyotes raise pup in dens?
    - A. to get closer to dangerous animals
    - B. because there is always food in a den
    - C. so the pups can grow up in a safe place

Answer key on page 24.

Glossary

adapted
Changed over time to deal with a certain situation.

camouflage
Colors that make an animal difficult to see in the area around it.

jaws
The two large bones that form an animal's mouth.

litter
A group of babies born to a mother at one time.

mammals
Animals that have hair and feed their babies milk.

mate
To come together to make a baby.

populations
The numbers of animals living in certain areas.

prairies
Huge, natural grasslands.

prey
Animals that are eaten by other animals.

shelter
Protection from danger or weather.

To Learn More

BOOKS

Chang, Kirsten. *Wolf or Coyote?* Minneapolis: Bellwether Media, 2020.

Olson, Elsie. *Animal Predator Smackdown.* Minneapolis: Abdo Publishing, 2020.

NOTE TO EDUCATORS

Visit **www.focusreaders.com** to find lesson plans, activities, links, and other resources related to this title.

Index

C
camouflage, 13

D
dens, 7, 19, 21

J
jaws, 9

L
litter, 19

M
mate, 19–21

P
pups, 7, 19–21

Answer Key: **1.** Answers will vary; **2.** Answers will vary; **3.** C; **4.** C